EXTREME

Extreme
Motorbikes

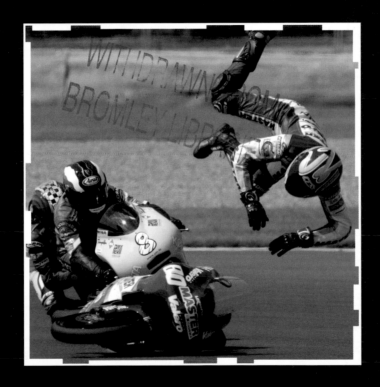

Clive Gifford

A ... on

Produced for A & C Black by
Monkey Puzzle Media Ltd
48 York Avenue
Hove BN3 1JD, UK

Published by A & C Black Publishers Limited
36 Soho Square, London W1D 3QY

Paperback published 2010
First published 2009

ISBN 978-1-4081-1474-2 (hardback)
ISBN 978-1-4081-1985-3 (paperback)

A CIP catalogue record for this book is available from the British Library.

Editor: Susie Brooks
Design: Mayer Media Ltd
Picture research: Lynda Lines
Series consultants: Jane Turner and James de Winter

This book is produced using paper that is made from wood grown in managed, sustainable forests. It is natural, renewable and recyclable. The logging and manufacturing processes conform to the environmental regulations of the country of origin.

Printed in Malaysia by Tien Wah Press (Pte.) Ltd

Picture acknowledgements
Action Images pp. 1 (Reuters/John Pryke), 11 (Reuters/Michael Kooren), 14 (Steven Paston), 16 (Sporting Pictures), 16–17 (Sporting Pictures), 18 (MSI), 19 (Reuters/John Pryke); Action Plus p. 13 (Leo Mason); A2 Wind Tunnel LLC p. 10; Corbis pp. 6 (Patrick Bennett), 8 (John W Gertz/zefa), 9 (Leah Warkentin/Design Pics), 22 (Lefevre/ASA/epa), 25 (Jens Wolf/epa); Getty Images pp. 5, 7 (Bongarts), 15 (Mario Laporta/AFP), 20 (Pascal Rondeau/Allsport), 20–21 (Mike Cooper/Allsport), 23 (Digital Vision), 24 (Volker Hartmann/AFP), 26 (Raveendran/AFP), 27 (Tony Ashby/AFP); MPM Images p. 28; New Zealand MiniMoto Race Club p. 4; Rocky-Robinson.com p. 29; Zodiac Drag Race Team p. 12 (Stefan Boman).

The front cover shows MotoGP drivers Nicky Hayden and Loris Capirossi at the Indianapolis Motor Speedway in Indiana, USA (Corbis/Tannen Maury/epa).

CONTENTS

Abbreviations km stands for kilometres • **m** stands for metres • **ft** stands for feet •
km/h stands for kilometres per hour • **mph** stands for miles per hour

Extreme machines

Imagine riding a motorbike that's twice as fast as your family's car – maybe even faster! Roaring beneath you is a power-packed engine that can whizz you up to top speed in seconds. Hold on tight!

The Suzuki Hayabusa is one of the fastest, meanest machines around. It's a super-fast bike, with a big engine creating enormous power. Its top speed is limited by law to 297 kilometres per hour (185 miles per hour) – but it can go faster!

In 2008, Trillium Muir became the world's fastest woman on a bike. Her Hayabusa reached almost 383 kilometres per hour (238 miles per hour). You have to be an expert rider to handle that sort of awesome power.

Even these tiny pocketbikes can reach around 90 km/h (56 mph)!

accelerate to increase speed

Vrmm, vrmm

The Hayabusa engine is so powerful that it has been used as the engine in a sports car – the Westfield Megabusa.

*A Suzuki Hayabusa can **accelerate** from 0 to 100 km/h (62.5 mph) in just 2.7 seconds!*

Tyre spins on road surface, causing **friction**.

Powerful engine drives the rear wheel round.

Friction produces heat – and lots of smoke!

Wheel spins.

friction the force that slows movement between two objects rubbing together

Start your engines

When you ride a motorbike, you're riding a kind of bomb! Explosions are going off many times a second inside a motorbike engine.

Twist and burn

Riders change their bike's speed using the **throttle**. This is usually a twist grip on the handlebar. It controls how much air is let into the engine's cylinders.

A motorbike engine has one or more **cylinders**. A precise amount of fuel and air are let into each cylinder. All it needs is a spark to make the mixture explode. This comes from an electrical part called a spark plug.

The explosion pushes a rod called a piston along the cylinder. This movement provides the energy to turn the bike's rear wheel round.

The rider's-eye view: the top dial shows the bike's speed. The bottom dial is a rev counter, which shows how fast the engine is working.

cylinder a tube in an engine where the power is created

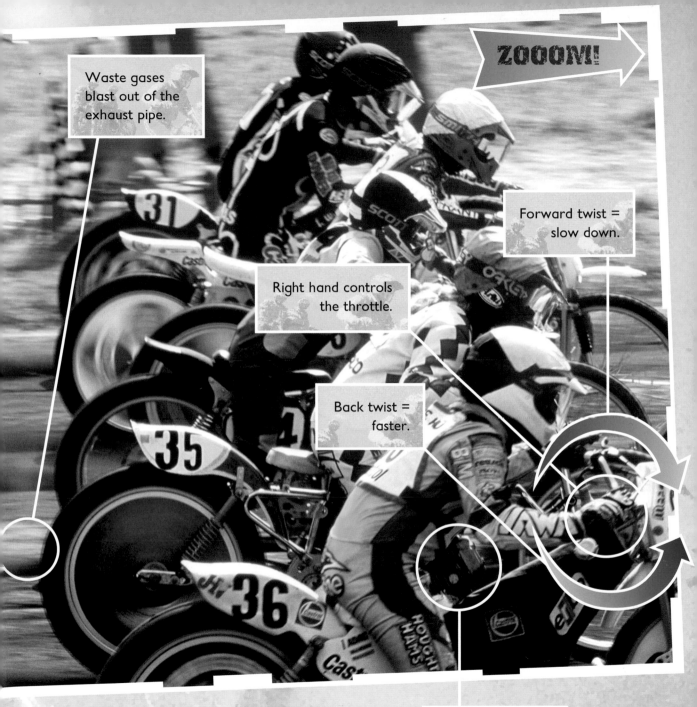

ZOOOM!

Waste gases blast out of the exhaust pipe.

Forward twist = slow down.

Right hand controls the throttle.

Back twist = faster.

Six racers speed away on their dirt-track bikes.

throttle a device for controlling speed

Fuel and air burn in the engine.

Wheelies!

Some riders reckon that two wheels are one too many. They use the power of the engine to lift the bike's front wheel off the ground. It's called "pulling a wheelie".

When you start a motorbike normally, both tyres grip the ground and the bike moves forwards on two wheels. But if the amount of power is suddenly increased, the rear wheel thrusts ahead and the front wheel rears up in the air. This is a wheelie.

Careful…that rear wheel is digging itself deeper into the desert!

The rider ends a wheelie by decreasing power, which shifts the bike's weight back over the front wheel. Then it's up to **gravity** to pull the wheel to the ground.

Wheeeeeelie!

In 1984, Doug Domokos kept a wheelie going for a staggering 232 kilometres (144 miles).

gravity a force that attracts objects to each other

8

Too much lean or power, and it's crash time!

Front wheel lifts.

Bike moves forwards.

Wheel turns.

Tyre grips the ground.

This looks like wheelie good fun — but don't try it at home!

The world's fastest race bikes

The biggest, baddest race bikes of all are **MotoGP** machines. No expense is spared on these amazing two-wheeled rocket ships.

A MotoGP bike can travel so fast, it's a wonder the wind doesn't knock the rider's head off! MotoGP racers have to tuck themselves out of the wind, or they wouldn't be able to hold on to the handlebars.

MotoGP bikes are designed to slice through the air as smoothly as possible. The bikes are made narrow, with parts tucked in. The rider "tucks in" too, hunched over the fuel tank.

Record racer

During the 2008 Shanghai Grand Prix MotoGP race, Casey Stoner's Ducati reached a record speed of 347 kilometres per hour (215.62 miles per hour).

A race bike is tested in a wind tunnel. Giant fans blast air over the motorbike, as if it is moving fast.

streamlined shaped so that air flows easily over it

10

This bike is **streamlined** to cut through the air as smoothly as possible.

Narrow handlebars keep the rider's hands and arms tucked in.

Rider tucks behind the **fairing**.

AIR FLOW

Engine is hidden behind the fairing.

Fairing smooths the air flow around the bike.

fairing a covering that protects from wind and helps with streamlining

Six-second sizzlers

MotoGP not fast enough for you? Try riding a top-fuel drag bike – it feels like having your arms pulled from their sockets!

Pairs of drag bikes race each other along a short, straight piece of track called a drag strip. Don't blink if you're watching – the race will be over in just 6 seconds!

Drag bikes are fitted with incredibly powerful engines. Their top speed is over 350 kilometres per hour (217 miles per hour). Keeping control is a tough task. A long arm called a wheelie bar is fitted to the back of the bike, to stop it doing a massive wheelie.

A drag bike spins its rear wheel before racing. "Burnouts" like this heat the back tyre, giving it more grip.

Gas guzzlers

Top-fuel bikes use a fuel called nitromethane instead of petrol. They use a lot – in fact, 40 litres (11 gallons) per kilometre raced!

drag bike a fast motorbike raced on a short, straight track

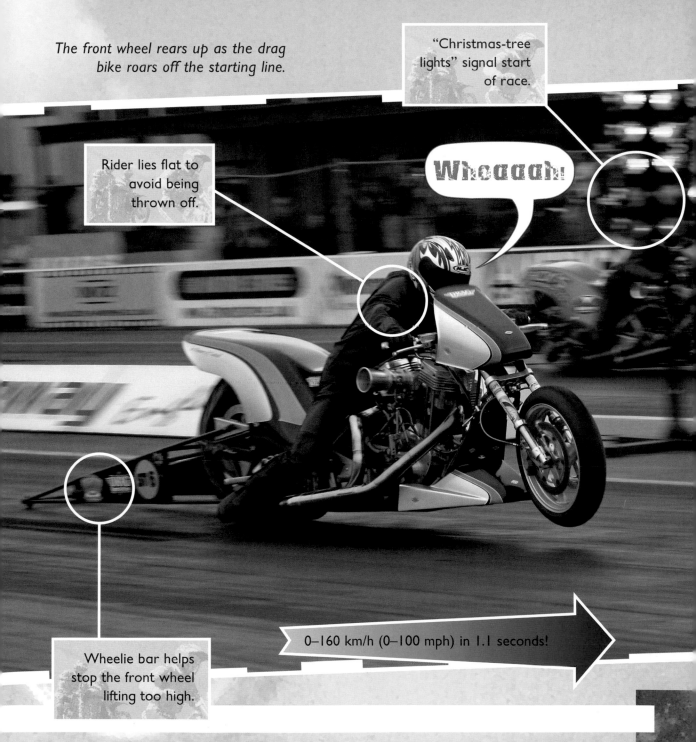

The front wheel rears up as the drag bike roars off the starting line.

"Christmas-tree lights" signal start of race.

Rider lies flat to avoid being thrown off.

Wheaaah!

Wheelie bar helps stop the front wheel lifting too high.

0–160 km/h (0–100 mph) in 1.1 seconds!

Cornering kings

Top bike racers can take corners faster than most people drive in a straight line! How on earth do their tyres grip the track?

Speedway bikes have no brakes! Riders use the throttle to get the back of the bike to drift sideways through the turn.

The tyres grip because they are made of special soft rubber. The weight of the bike and rider pushes the tyre against the track surface. A force called friction allows the tyre to take hold. Imagine a motorbike tyre made of something slippery, like glass. It wouldn't work very well!

Touch down

Only a small part of each tyre touches the ground at one time. This is called the contact patch. Incredibly, the contact patch for each tyre is no bigger than a credit card.

speedway racing on an oval-shaped dirt track

Valentino Rossi leads a race through a pair of turns. Mid-turn, the riders' knees skim the ground — or even scrape it.

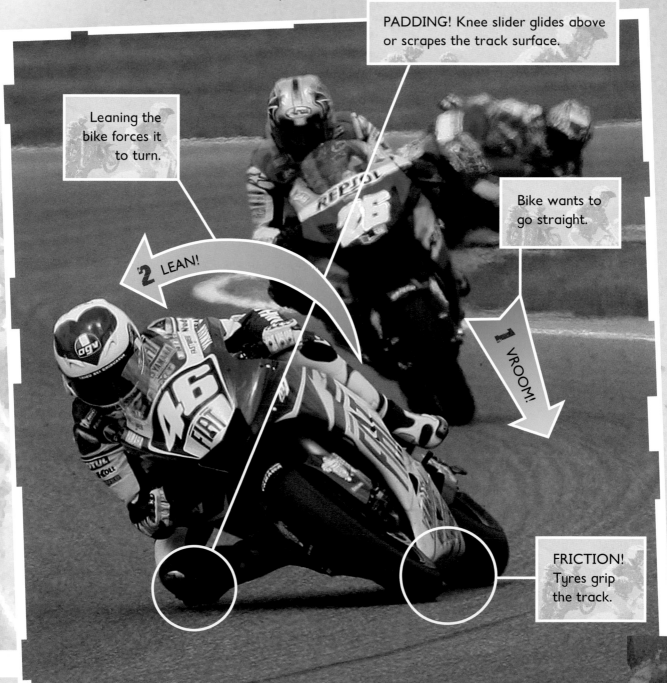

PADDING! Knee slider glides above or scrapes the track surface.

Leaning the bike forces it to turn.

Bike wants to go straight.

2 LEAN!

1 VROOM!

FRICTION! Tyres grip the track.

Gripping stuff

Motorbikes on ice? No kidding. Ice speedway is a serious sport with its own World Championships. The secret is in the special tyres, which provide grip on the most slippery of surfaces.

Ice speedway bikes race around short, oval tracks. They have just enough fuel in their tiny tanks for four laps of the track. But there's nothing else puny about these machines!

The bikes reach 130 kilometres per hour (81 miles per hour) on the short straights, and barely slow down for each tight, icy bend. The spikes on their wheels dig into the ice, which produces the grip needed to race on ice.

Protective guard stops the wheel spiking other riders.

Ouch! Ninety sharp steel spikes on the front wheel (the rear has 200–500!).

Baling out

If they lose it, ice speedway riders hit a piled-up snow bank or straw bales on the outside edge of the track.

Spikes dig in for extreme grip.

Speed around bend = 90–100 km/h (56–62 mph)

GRIP

SPEED

Ice speedway riders take every corner with extreme lean.
Their knees and handlebars just brush the ice!

CRASH!

Most of the time, grip (or friction) is a rider's friend, keeping the tyres steady. But once in a while, grip goes wrong and turns out to be a rider's enemy...

These riders are performing a "stoppie". Using the front brake hard stops the front wheel, but the back wheel keeps moving and lifts up!

Air bag

The Honda Goldwing GL1800 has an **airbag** to protect a rider's head. In a front-on crash, the bag inflates in 0.06 seconds.

One of the most spectacular crashes you can have is a "highside". This happens when the rear tyre loses grip in a corner. The back of the bike starts to slide sideways. It's embarrassing, but not disastrous – unless the back tyre grips the track again. The bike suddenly stops sliding and trips over, flinging the rider into the air.

airbag an inflatable cushion that protects a driver in a crash

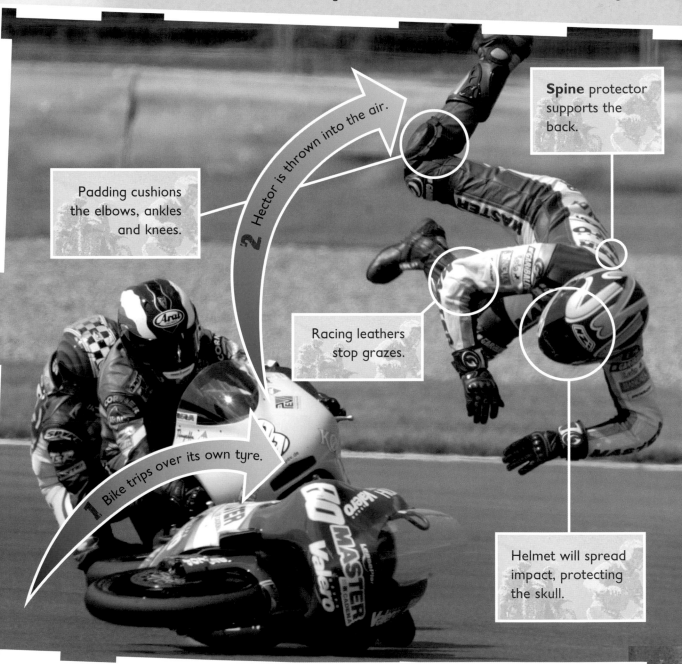

Sixteen-year-old Hector Barbera flies through the air at the 2002 British 125cc Grand Prix. He walked away from this crash, and won the race the next year.

Spine protector supports the back.

Padding cushions the elbows, ankles and knees.

2 Hector is thrown into the air.

Racing leathers stop grazes.

1 Bike trips over its own tyre.

Helmet will spread impact, protecting the skull.

spine the backbone

Sidecar racer

Passengers on extreme sidecar race bikes don't just sit there. They're expected to help the driver by leaning out over the track, skimming its surface!

Weight over the back wheel = more grip = more speed!

Sidecar passengers are known as "monkeys", for the way they scramble all over the vehicle. They do this because sidecars don't lean into turns like regular motorbikes. Instead, they enter the turn upright, and the monkey shifts his or her body weight to keep the sidecar from flipping up. When there is a series of left and right turns, a monkey has to move fast!

Sidecar star

Steve Webster is the most successful sidecar racer ever. He has won ten Sidecar World Championships. In 181 races, he finished in the top three 131 times.

sidecar a one-wheeled attachment to a bike, allowing a passenger

A sidecar enters a left turn at the famous Nürburgring track in Germany.

Rough riders

Motorbikes are not just ridden at extreme speeds. They are ridden in extreme places too. Welcome to the world of the rough riders – where bumps, jumps and dirt are guaranteed.

Off-road riding is a dangerous sport. Broken bones are common, and even top riders sometimes have to miss races because they are injured. The best racer ever, Ricky Carmichael, had to sit out the whole 2005 **supercross** season because he was injured.

To help with rocky rides, off-road bikes need good **suspension**. This lessens the shock of the impact when a bike goes over a bump or lands from a jump.

Over 1,000 rough riders tackle the crazy Enduro du Touquet race. The race is 16 km (10 miles) long over massive sand dunes.

GOAT

Ricky Carmichael's nickname was GOAT (Greatest Of All Time)! In 2002, he recorded the first-ever "perfect season" – a race season in which he was unbeaten in any race. Then he did it again in 2004!

supercross off-road racing using specialized, high-performance bikes

Motocross riders nail a jump.

Suspension spring softens landing.

Front fork telescopes in and then out to absorb impact.

BOING!

Bike powers away so it doesn't get bogged down.

THROTTLE ON!

suspension a system of shock absorbers designed to reduce bumps

BIG beasts

Some bikes are big – really BIG! The biggest factory-produced motorbikes weigh about six times as much as an average man. But some one-off machines are much larger.

Tall order

Dream Big took Gregory Dunham three years to build. The enormous handlebars are just for show. The real steering is done using a car steering wheel!

Designers normally try to keep the weight of their motorbikes low. Less weight helps a bike to move faster and use less fuel. But Tilo Niebel wasn't worried about weight when he built the *Harzer Bike Schmiede*.

With a height of 3.429 m (11.25 ft), Dream Big is the world's tallest motorcycle.

Harzer Bike Schmiede is the world's heaviest motorcycle-sidecar. It weighs 4,749 kilograms (748 stone) — more than twenty-one Suzuki Hayabusas!

The Harzer Bike Schmiede's *engine comes from a Russian T55 tank and has twelve cylinders — six times as many as some bikes!*

Russian tank badge

Old searchlight as front headlight

Almost 3 m (10 ft) wide

Over 5 m (16 ft) long

Sidecar is built from the front of an old Russian truck.

Tyres are over 1 m (3 ft) tall.

Biking on air

Most bikers are keen to stay in their seats. But there's one breed of biker that thinks a ride spent seated is a dull one indeed – the freestyle motocross rider!

Freestyle motocross is often called FMX. The riders launch their bikes way up into the air, high enough to jump through a first-floor window. Not content with daredevil leaps, they started inventing crazy tricks in mid-air, including:

- **Backflip** (single or double) – bike and rider do one or two full backward rotations.
- **Can can** – rider lifts a foot over the seat and back again.
- **Superman seatgrab** – rider gets off the bike in mid-air, holding on only to the seat, legs sticking straight out behind.

WEIGHT

WEIGHT

Weight has to be evenly balanced.

Thirteen on a single bike – surely that's against the law? These men should know... they're all from the Indian Police!

Daredevil Robbie Maddison momentarily lets go of his bike in mid-air during the Gravity Games in Perth, Australia.

Rider and bike move at the same speed.

As long as the rider doesn't push the bike away from him, it's safe to let go.

Bike moves through the air.

Big air

Australian stunt rider Robbie Maddison gained **REALLY** big air in 2008. His world motorbike jump record was a whopping 106.98 metres (351 feet).

Record breakers

This is it, the ultimate test of motorbike muscle – the World Motorcycle Land Speed Record. Since 2006, it's been a head-to-head battle between two monstrous machines.

Round One went to Rocky Robinson riding the *Top 1 Oil Ack Attack*. In September 2006, it reached a staggering 551.7 kilometres per hour (342.8 miles per hour). Two days later, Chris Carr on the *Bub Lucky 7* topped it with 564.7 kilometres per hour (350.9 miles per hour). Ouch!

Rocky and his team licked their wounds and tried again in 2008. The end result: 580.8 kilometres per hour (360.9 miles per hour). Now that's *extreme*!

In 1907, Glenn Curtiss built his own bike with no brakes and reached 219 km/h (136 mph). No motorbike would go faster until 1930.

Blind Ninja

In 2003, Billy Baxter created a new blind world speed record of 265.33 kilometres per hour (164.9 miles per hour), riding a Kawasaki Ninja while wearing a blindfold.

The Bub Lucky 7 *(back) and* Top 1 Oil Ack Attack *line up on Bonneville Salt Flats, USA, ready for record-breaking extreme-speed action.*

carbon fibre a lightweight but very strong material

Glossary

accelerate to increase speed

airbag an inflatable cushion that protects a driver in a crash

carbon fibre a lightweight but very strong material

cylinder a tube in an engine where the power is created

drag bike a fast motorbike raced on a short, straight track

fairing a covering that protects from wind and helps with streamlining

friction the force that slows movement between two objects rubbing together

gravity a force that attracts objects to each other

sidecar a one-wheeled attachment to a bike, allowing a passenger

speedway racing on an oval-shaped dirt track

spine the backbone

streamlined shaped so that air flows easily over it

supercross off-road racing using specialized, high-performance bikes

suspension a system of shock absorbers designed to reduce bumps

throttle a device for controlling speed

Further information

Books

The Illustrated Encyclopedia of Motorcycles by Roland Brown (Southwater, 2007)
Learn all about more than 200 makes of bikes in this photo-packed book.

Motorbikes by Chris Oxlade (Franklin Watts, 2006)
Lots of information on some of the biggest and fastest motorbikes around.

Motocross by Paul Mason (Wayland, 2008)
All you need to know about the extreme sport of motocross.

The Need For Speed: Motorbikes by Philip Raby & Simon Nix (Franklin Watts, 2000)
Found in libraries and on the Internet, a great book on extreme motorcycles and races.

Magazines

There are dozens of motorbike mags out there covering every type of motorbike. In the USA, **Cycle World**, **Roadracing World** and **Dirt Rider** are popular while **Transworld Motocross** is the biggest motocross mag on the planet. In the UK, **Bike** and the newspaper **MCN** are both popular, while **Motorcycle Racer** is great for road and track racing. Top Australian mags include **Two Wheels**, **Heavy Duty** and **ADB** (**Australasian Dirt Bike**).

Websites

http://motorcycleviews. com
Head to the FAQs for Non-riders and you'll find some very useful webpages describing how motorbikes and their parts work.

www.motogp.com
Check out dozens of videos of MotoGP action and learn about the bikes and riders at this official website.

www.motorcycle-usa. com
A top American website packed with news, race results and features on all kinds of bikes.

www.freestyle motocrossteamfmx.com
Watch some great motocross and stunt riding videos at Team FMX East's website.

Film

Faster directed by Mark Neale (Dorna Sports, 2003)
Narrated by motorcycle-mad actor, Ewan McGregor, this exciting documentary tells the story of the MotoGP championship.

Index